WARFARE!

WARFARE!

MOIRA BUTTERFIELD

FRANKLIN WATTS
LONDON • SYDNEY

Weird True Facts! the boring stuff...

First published in 2012 by Franklin Watts
Copyright © Franklin Watts 2012
Franklin Watts
338 Euston Road
London NW1 3BH

Franklin Watts Australia
Level 17/207 Kent Street
Sydney, NSW 2000

A CIP catalogue record for this book
is available from the British Library.

Dewey no: 355'.02

ISBN: 978 1 4451 0481 2

Printed in China

Franklin Watts is a division of Hachette Children's Books,
an Hachette UK company
www.hachette.co.uk

Series editor: Sarah Ridley
Editor in Chief: John C. Miles
Designer: www.rawshock.co.uk/Jason Anscomb
Art director: Jonathan Hair
Picture research: Diana Morris
Artwork: Lee Montgomery

Picture credits: AMC Photography/Shutterstock: front cover br, 14.
Yuri Beletsky/ESO: 28c. Lance Bellers/istockphoto: 13tl. Bettmann/Corbis: 19t, 23t.
G. Blakeley/istockphoto: front cover t, 21b. British Library Images, London: 16tl.
Neal Coulsand/Shutterstock: 15tr. Jack Cronkhite/Shutterstock: 6t.
Janaka Dhamasena/Shutterstock: 20t. Mary Evans PL/Alamy: 19b.
filmfoto/Shutterstock: 10tr. FWA: 7b, 17t.General Dynamics Electric Boat/US Navy: 25b.
Alex Gul/Shutterstock: 29b.Victor Habbick/SPL: 27t. Hisamikabunomura/Wikipe-
dia Commons: 17b. Hulton Archive/Getty Images: 21b. JPL/Caltech/NASA: 29tr. JPL/
Caltech/Stsci/NASA: 29tl. Nik Keevil/Alamy: 9b. Capt. Patricia Lang/USAF: front cover
c, 23b. Lockheed Martin: 26t. Mass Communication Specialist 3rd Class Travis K.
Mendoza/US Navy: 25t. Musée de l'Armee, Paris: 16b. Musée du Louvre, Paris/
Superstock: front cover bl, 11b. NASA: 28t. National Archives/Heritage Images/Topfoto:
18b. Pete Ryan/Alamy: 22. Science & Society PL/Getty Images: 20b. sspopov/
Shutterstock: 15bl. Superstock: 13tr. Geoff Tomkinson/SPL: 27b. Travelshots/Superstock:
10tl. US Army: 26b. V & A, London/Superstock: 11t. Viva-Verdi.CC Wikipedia: 24.
Waj/Shutterstock: 12

Every attempt has been made to clear copyright. Should there be any
inadvertent omission please apply to the publisher for rectification.

CONTENTS

 ## ANCIENT BATTLES

For centuries people have been fighting for land and power throughout the world. Here are some of the earliest examples of warfare.

The Chinese 'Terracotta Army' — clay models of an ancient army dating from 200 BCE.

EARLY WARFARE

3300 BCE
Prehistoric tribes fought with bows and spears. The frozen body of a 5,000-year-old Stone Age man, with an arrow wound in his shoulder, was discovered in the European Alps in 1991.

1475 BCE
The first battle ever recorded, the Battle of Megiddo (in modern-day Israel) was fought between ancient Egyptian Pharaoh Thutmose III and a rebel army.

911–605 BCE
The Assyrians developed fighting with chariots. They had an ancient empire in modern-day Iraq and the Middle East.

800 BCE
Indian armies used war elephants in battle. Fierce males captured from the wild made the best elephant warriors.

400 BCE (exact date unknown)
Chinese General Sun Tzu wrote *The Art of War*, a combat manual still read by modern commanders.

210–209 BCE
Chinese emperor Qin Shi Huang was buried with around 8,000 life-size clay warriors, in case he had to fight battles in the afterlife.

TOUGHEST FIGHTERS EVER

Between 600–400 BCE the city-state of Sparta in ancient Greece trained all its males to be vicious warriors. If a Spartan baby looked too weak to be a warrior, it was thrown over a cliff. At the age of seven all Spartan boys left home and began brutal army training. At 12, they were sent to live in wild countryside on their own for a year, with only one piece of clothing, no shoes and no food stores. If they survived, they had no choice but to live their life in the Spartan army.

Soldiers in ancient Sparta wore a crested helmet and leg armour. They carried a heavy shield to protect themselves.

Archimedes' 'death ray' may have focused the rays of the Sun onto enemy ships, to set them on fire.

Weapons wonder

Famous inventor Archimedes (287–212 BCE) developed some of the world's first war machines to protect his home town of Syracuse (in the region of modern Sicily) from Roman attack. He designed a giant rock-launching catapult and a mechanical claw which could stretch out over the city walls, hook onto enemy ships and capsize them. He is also said to have invented a 'death ray' which focused rays of sunlight onto ships, setting fire to them.

ROMANS RULE!

The Roman army controlled Europe and North Africa for 600 years (roughly 200 BCE to 400 CE). It was the most powerful fighting force in the ancient western world.

Legionaries wore heavy protective metal helmets. Officers' helmets had a plume on the top.

Under his *lorica* (iron armour), a legionary wore a woollen tunic and a linen vest.

In addition to a *pilum* (javelin), a Roman soldier carried a *gladius* (short sword).

A Roman legionary's *scutum* (shield) was decorated with patterns representing his legion.

RANKING ROMANS

The army was organised into legions – groups of 5,000 soldiers. Here are a few of the people you might come across in a legion:

Legate The commander, usually a wealthy nobleman who didn't actually fight but wore ceremonial chest armour shaped to make him look as if he had big muscles.

Centurion Commander of an 80-man group called a century. He wore a helmet with feathers on top and carried a staff (big stick) to beat lazy soldiers.

Legionary An ordinary foot soldier who joined up for 25 years and swore an oath to fight to the death.

Aquilifer The soldier who carried the Legion's standard, a carved symbol on a pole. It was a terrible disgrace to lose it.

Signifer The soldier who carried the centurial *signum*, a spear hung with medallions (left). Soldiers rallied around it in battle.

Cornicen A horn player who blasted out the commander's signals to the troops.

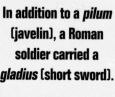

Roman warfare facts

- Roman enemies, the Celts, sometimes fought naked.

- The Carthaginians fought the Romans using war elephants. The Romans discovered that the elephants were scared of squealing pigs, so they covered pigs in tar, set light to them and let them loose during battles.

- Before battles, German tribes tried to scare their Roman enemy with out-of-tune chanting.

- Roman soldiers weren't allowed to get married, but they could have girlfriends and families.

- In cold weather Roman soldiers wore socks with their sandals.

- The standard bearers wore animal skins on top of their uniforms.

This signifer carries a standard with the symbol of his legion — a mythical seahorse.

Roman re-enactors prepare to fire some seriously big arrows from a reconstructed ballista.

WAR MACHINES, ROMAN-STYLE

The Roman army had some powerful wooden war machines that their enemies couldn't match. They might use a ballista (left) to fire metal bolts or big arrows at enemy troops, or they might try an onager, a giant catapult that could lob large stones at enemy defences.

Some you lose

The Roman army did have a few disasters. The Carthaginians defeated them in 217 BCE at the Battle of Lake Trasimene, one of the biggest ambushes in military history. Hannibal hid his army behind hills and then surprised the Roman forces, killing over 15,000 of them. In 9 CE, 25,000 Roman soldiers were killed by local warrior tribes in the marshy Teutoburg Forest (now part of Germany). They were lured into a trap and ambushed.

FOUR-LEGGED FIGHTERS

ENTER THE HORSE

Up until the 1900s horses were a vital part of war. Here are some of the best four-legged fighters in history.

Re-enactors recreate the Battle of Hastings, fought in 1066. Mounted knights won the day.

Knights were fond of jousting – charging at an opponent and trying to knock him off his horse.

NORMANS ON TOP

Date 1066

Warriors The Normans invaded England from France.

How horses helped A new invention – stirrups – meant the Normans could stay mounted on horseback during battle. They used long lances to spear the enemy English, who fought on foot. Once the Normans ruled, life in England changed forever, so the battle victory was a major historical event.

MEDIEVAL MOUNTS

Date 1000–1500

Warriors Mounted knights fought battles in Medieval Europe.

How horses helped Knights wore heavy armour and needed a big strong war horse, called a destrier, to carry them.

Mounted Mongol cavalrymen, such as this one, terrified Asia and Eastern Europe in the 1200s.

HORSIE HOARDS

Date 1200s

Warriors The Mongols conquered Asia, the Middle East and parts of Europe. They were expert horsemen who could shoot arrows while galloping.

How horses helped The Mongol army could travel long distances very fast because each warrior had three or four horses and could swap between them as they got tired. If the army ran out of food, the troops drank mares' (female horses') milk and horses' blood.

SABRE-SLASHERS

Date 1800s

Warriors *Cuirassiers,* French cavalry who rode at the front of Napoleon's armies. They were famed throughout Europe.

How horses helped The cuirassiers thundered into enemy lines on horseback, slashing and smashing their way through using long sabres and pistols. They got their name from their breast plate, called a *cuirasse*.

Famous war horses

Alexander the Great (356-323 BCE) conquered parts of Europe and Asia on his war horse Bucephalus. He even named a city – Bucephala – after the horse, who eventually died in battle.

Napoleon, Emperor of France in the early 1800s, had a famous light grey war horse called Marengo, (right) which was wounded eight times in its war career. Its skeleton is on display at the National Army Museum in London.

Napoleon was finally defeated at Waterloo in 1815 by the Duke of Wellington, who rode a horse called Copenhagen. When the horse died of old age Wellington gave it a burial with full military honours.

NO, YOU CAN'T COME IN!

CASTLES AND SIEGES

Sieges have been used in warfare since ancient times, to try to force an enemy from an important town or fortress.

The walls contained hidden passages where defenders could hide.

There was a double ring of defensive walls and strong guard towers.

Archers could shoot at the enemy through narrow arrow slits.

There was room inside for 2,000 troops and 1,000 horses.

Krak des Chevaliers was built high on a cliff.

Between the inner and outer walls there was a zig-zag shaped ramp entrance, which could be easily defended.

Parts of the inner wall were over 30m thick.

There were underground storage rooms for food and weaponry.

CRACK CASTLE

Castles were medieval fortified bases built to withstand enemy sieges. The huge fortress of Krak des Chevaliers in Syria, shown above, was built with many anti-siege features. A group of Christian knights occupied it from 1142, and the castle withstood many sieges before it was finally captured in 1271. The knights were tricked out of the castle by a forged letter from their commanders, ordering them to surrender.

A trebuchet uses the power of a falling counterweight to fling rocks at castle walls. This is a modern reconstruction.

Castle defenders throw rocks down on besiegers in this old engraving.

How to besiege

Here are some medieval methods of attacking a castle:

- Block food supplies and poison the water supply, or bribe a defender to let you in.

- Fling stones at the walls or dig tunnels under them to make them collapse.

- Climb up wooden siege towers, which looked like giant four-sided ladders, to get onto the walls.

How to keep besiegers out

Here are tactics used to withstand a siege:

- Destroy all the farmland around. That way the besiegers might run out of food first.

- Stop tunnels being dug under your walls. In the 400s, Chinese defenders used giant bellows to pump smoke into tunnels dug by attackers.

- Drop boiling liquid or stones on attackers over the walls or through 'murder holes' – holes in the ceiling of the castle entrance.

BUILDING UP TO VICTORY

In 332 BCE Greek leader Alexander the Great (see p11) besieged the city of Tyre, which stood on an island. He eventually conquered it by building a giant causeway across the sea to the island. Then he sold its 30,000 residents into slavery.

In 52 BCE Roman leader Julius Caesar built two walls around the camp of his Gaulish enemy Vercingetorix, at the Siege of Alesia. The walls trapped the Gauls in and stopped them getting supplies. Eventually the starving Gauls tried to fight their way out, but the Romans won.

ARMOURED DEFENCE

Since very early times soldiers have tried to protect themselves from harm by dressing in different types of armour. Here are some examples of their attempts.

ARMOUR TIMELINE

1500 BCE

Before metal was discovered, warriors made do with animal hides. Some ancient Chinese warriors wore armour made from turtle shells tied together with cord; others wore tunics made of rhinoceros hide.

400–300 BCE

Ancient Greek hoplite warriors wore some body armour, including helmets, bronze breastplates and greaves (shin guards).

200 BCE–500 CE

The Romans wore a helmet and flexible chest armour made of metal bands tied together.

500 CE–1200 CE

Chainmail was created by riveting together hundreds of tiny metal rings, but it took a lot of time and effort and was expensive.

The best way to kill a knight in armour was to hit him hard with a mace (iron club), or stick a dagger or spear through any gaps.

Suits of armour were expensive, and only for the wealthy.

Knights wore linen or woolly underclothes under their armour.

Knights still had to wear some chainmail to protect parts of the body that armour would not fit, such as the backs of the knees.

1200s CE–1500s CE

Iron plating was cheaper and easier to make than chainmail. By 1400 knights wore complete suits of armour and their horses wore armour, too. A full medieval suit of armour was heavy, weighing around 27kg (60 lb), but modern soldiers carry backpacks that are heavier.

1600s–1800s

The development of guns made armour less effective. Soldiers wore less and less – usually only back and breast (chest) plates.

1800s

Nineteenth century Japanese Samurai warriors wore an armoured skirt and other ceremonial armour made of metal plates tied together. Their helmet was meant to make them look scary.

This ceremonial Samurai armour includes an impressive fake moustache and horns fixed onto the Darth-Vader style helmet.

Ned Kelly's homemade armour.

Kabuto
(helmet)

Kusazuri
(armoured skirt)

1880

Australian outlaw Ned Kelly and his gang made their own armour to protect themselves in a shootout with police. The police wounded Ned by shooting his legs, and he was captured and hanged. His famous homemade armour is now on display in Melbourne.

1900s–2000s

Metal armour does not offer good protection from bullets. Modern soldiers wear bulletproof padded vests made from light but very strong material such as Kevlar ™.

ARTILLERY ARRIVES

The invention of gunpowder made a big difference to the way wars were fought.

This Chinese illustration shows a footsoldier using a firelance.

Powerful powder

Gunpowder was probably invented in China in the 800s CE. It was used to power flamethrowers called firelances and gunpowder rockets, sometimes shaped like dragons.

Legend has it that the Chinese discovered gunpowder accidentally, while experimenting to make an immortality potion.

In early medieval Europe gunpowder was used in weapons that shot out Greek Fire, a mixture of flaming chemicals that could even burn underwater.

WAR GETS LOADED

Early cannons were used in the 1200s CE to fire stone cannonballs at castle walls. They were difficult to operate and sometimes exploded, killing everyone around them.

This painting, dating from the 1400s, shows attackers firing early cannons at a castle wall.

The biggest gun ever made was *Schwer Gustav*, built in 1941 for use by German forces in World War Two. Its huge shells could make 9m-wide craters up to 37km away.

GUNS AND WARFARE

The musket was the type of gun used by footsoldiers between the 1500s and the 1700s. It was only effective if lots of muskets were fired at the enemy at once.

Hiram Maxim invented the first portable automatic machine gun in 1884, firing a continuous stream of bullets.

Gunners often gave their weapons names. *Big Bertha* and *Schwer* (heavy) *Gustav*, shown above, were names given to World War Two artillery guns.

In 2010 the US Navy tested a new type of supergun – the electromagnetic railgun – that does not need gunpowder. Instead a giant surge of electromagnetic energy shoots a set of rails forward, firing a missile at an incredible 9,072km/hr.

GUN BARREL BASICS

In the 1700s new ways of loading and 'rifling' (cutting grooves inside the gun barrel) led to the invention of rifles, which fired elongated bullets and were more accurate than muskets.

This picture shows the inside of a rifled gun barrel, with the grooves spiralling round towards the muzzle, or front. The bullet runs between the grooves and spins, giving it more power and accuracy.

WINNING BATTLES

Winning a battle takes good organisation, and you need lots of different types of people in your army.

Beware of spies

Spies are vital for gathering information about an enemy's battle plans, but one of the biggest Allied successes in World War Two relied on fooling spies. The Allies were planning to invade France via Normandy, but wanted the Germans to think they were going to land elsewhere. They faked radio messages and plans, and even parked fake landing craft at a British port to fool German spies. The information led to the Germans setting up defences in the wrong place.

HOW TO WIN

How? To win a battle, a military force needs a plan – an 'order of battle' – so they know where their forces and equipment are and how they will fight.

Where? An army's position on the battlefield is vital. Being on top of a hill is ideal, for instance, because the enemy has to come up hill to fight.

Who? Armies are organised into different sections such as regiments and companies, each with its own senior officers. Commanders can then give orders to different parts of their force.

These fake tanks were set up by British forces before D-Day in 1944 to fool German spies.

TOUGH TACTICS

Ancient Greek armies (2500 BCE – 200 BCE) used a troop formation called the 'phalanx'. Groups of footsoldiers packed together in a rectangle shape. Phalanxes would attack each other, trying to break up the enemy's shape.

In the 1700s and 1800s armies would use cavalry to charge enemy formations and quickly exploit weaknesses. On the battlefield, trumpet signals were used to give orders to the cavalry.

In World War Two German forces used a battle tactic called *blitzkrieg*. It relied on moving fast and surprising the enemy, first with a heavy bombardment of artillery, then with aerial fighter and bomber attacks, and finally with tanks.

The Charge of the Light Brigade, in 1854. The cavalrymen rode straight towards the Russian guns.

Infamous disasters

1066 At the Battle of Hastings the English army of King Harold was in a strong position on a hill but their enemy, the Normans, faked a retreat. The English broke ranks and ran down the hill after them. Then the Normans turned and fought back, killing Harold.

1854 118 men were killed in the Charge of the Light Brigade, when a badly worded order was misunderstood and a British cavalry unit charged up the wrong valley, directly into fire from Russian artillery.

TOP TANKS

Tanks became vital to warfare during the 1900s, and they are still used in modern combat.

EARLY IDEAS

In 1487 inventor Leonardo da Vinci sketched an armoured vehicle. He also sketched a type of machine gun, a parachute and a helicopter centuries before the concepts were actually developed.

In 1903 British novelist HG Wells published a short story called 'The Land Iron Clads', imagining a type of battle tank. His idea was taken up by engineers, who began developing tank designs.

The British shipped the first tanks out to France during World War One (1914–18). They labelled the cargo 'water tanks' to keep them a secret, and the name stuck.

Leonardo da Vinci's drawing of a tank.

WORLD WAR ONE

British Mark 1 tanks took part in the Battle of the Somme in 1916, the first tanks ever used in warfare. Inside they were unbearably hot and filled with exhaust fumes, and the crew of eight had to wear stifling chainmail masks to protect themselves from splinters of metal that flew off the walls when bullets hit the tank.

Towards the end of the war, the Germans designed their own giant tank, the A7V, which needed a crew of 18. The first ever tank-to-tank combat took place in 1918 between A7Vs and British tanks.

The huge, lumbering German A7V.

The Battle of Kursk was an epic struggle between tank forces.

How to stop tanks

Mines, missiles and obstacles were all developed to counter tanks in warfare. In World War Two anti-tank obstacles included 'dragon's teeth' – concrete pyramids set in the ground to stop tanks getting by.

WORLD WAR TWO

Tanks played a big part in World War Two. German forces used Panzer tanks in devastating blitzkrieg attacks (see p19). Some 6,000 tanks were involved in the Battle of Kursk in 1943, the biggest tank battle ever, between German Tiger and Panzer tanks against Russian T-34s.

The British modified some of their World War Two tanks in unusual ways. These included the Crocodile, which had a flamethrower instead of a gun, and the Bobbin, which could roll out a canvas path in front of it.

HI-TEC TANKS

Modern tanks are much lighter and more manoeuvrable than older versions. New developments include stealth technology to disguise tanks and 'reactive armour' which can explode an anti-tank charge on impact before it penetrates the tank shell.

Armed with a cannon and machine guns.

The M1A2 has computer-controlled navigation and communications.

The tank has infra-red sensors to navigate and target enemies at night.

It is fitted with protection from biological, chemical and nuclear attack.

The USA's M1A2 Abrams tank, used in modern warfare.

WAR IN THE AIR

In 1903 the Wright brothers made the first ever powered flight. It wasn't long before aeroplanes became an important weapon in warfare.

World War One pilots had no parachute to help them escape.

A reconstruction of the Red Baron's Fokker Dr 1 triplane, made of wood and canvas. He had it painted blood-red.

DOGFIGHTING DAYS

At the beginning of World War One aeroplanes were only used for reconnaissance. However, sometimes it was hard to spot things from above. One German observer reported that he had seen British troops running around panicking, when in fact they were playing football.

Soon, pilots on either side began shooting at each other with pistols and even throwing things such as grenades, bricks and ropes at enemy plane propellers.

Eventually the planes were fitted with onboard guns to become the first fighters, and the term 'dogfight' was first used to describe air combat between two planes.

Successful fighter pilots were called 'aces', and one of the most famous was German pilot Baron Manfred Von Richthofen, better known as the 'Red Baron'. He had 80 combat victories before he himself was killed.

JETS ARRIVE

Jet propulsion was first used to power aircraft during World War Two. The first jet in service was the German Messerschmitt 262. The first pilots who flew it were amazed by its speed. One even said it felt, "like angels pushing".

Pilots of the British Gloster Meteor jet were able to fly alongside German V1 flying bombs and tip them off-course with a nudge from the plane's wingtip.

Jet-engine basics

1. In jet engines air gets sucked in through the front into a compressor, a set of vanes that spin around and squeeze the air into the combustion chamber.

2. In the combustion chamber, the air mixes with fuel and is set alight. Hot gases shoot backwards, spinning turbine blades which turn the compressor. The gases rush out of the back of the engine at high speed, powering the plane forwards.

The F15 can carry air-to-air or air-to-ground weapons, including laser-guided or infra-red guided bombs.

Information for the pilot appears on a head-up display on the windscreen.

Today's fighter

Modern fighter jets have sophisticated equipment onboard. This F15 Eagle Fighter is in service with the US Air Force.

The F15 can climb 10,000m in around 60 seconds, and reach a speed of 3,017.52km/hr.

It can tow a fibre-optic decoy which confuses incoming radar-guided missiles by giving out a signal stronger than the plane itself.

Electronic systems provide threat detection and automatic countermeasures to combat incoming missiles.

FLOATING FORTRESSES

SAILING THROUGH HISTORY

400s BCE Ancient Greek navies used triremes, powered by around 170 oarsmen. The trireme had an underwater ram for smashing into enemy vessels.

1100s CE onwards The invention of gunpowder led to the development of warships armed with cannons.

1600s–1700s Naval tactics were based on the 'line of battle', a row of ships one behind the other, firing their cannons broadside (all at once) at the enemy.

1775 The first military submarine, the Turtle, was invented in the USA. It was shaped like a giant wooden acorn, with room for one person.

1800s Steam and diesel power developed along with metal hulls. Warships grew much bigger and heavier.

1900s Aircraft carriers and submarines became a vital part of modern warfare.

Ships have been used in warfare for thousands of years, as invasion transports and for fighting afloat.

THE LAST SURVIVOR

HMS *Victory*, docked in Portsmouth, England, is the oldest surviving warship still in use by any navy in the world. She was launched in 1765 and took part in lots of military action. She is still in commission and is used for British Royal Navy ceremonies.

At the Battle of Trafalgar in 1805 British Admiral Lord Nelson was onboard when the Napoleonic French and Spanish combined fleet was defeated. During the battle Nelson was shot by a French marksman and died below decks.

HMS *Victory* had over 100 cannons of different sizes. The heaviest guns were put on the lower decks, so the ship would not be top heavy.

The crew had a hard life, living in cramped conditions. Some were as young as eleven years old. They ate a diet of salted meat, maggot-filled ship's biscuits and a gallon of beer a day.

A view of the stern (back) of HMS *Victory*.

The USS *Nimitz* is a giant floating military airbase.

NUCLEAR-POWERED SUBMARINES

There are two types of nuclear-powered submarine. Attack submarines carry cruise missiles and torpedoes for attacking enemy ships. They are smaller and faster than missile submarines, which carry long-range nuclear missiles.

Length of mission Can stay submerged for up to 90 days, when they need to come up for more food supplies. They recycle their own air and water.

Sub length Attack subs are around 110m long. Missile subs are much longer, around 171m.

Possible depth of dive More than 290m, but exact figures are top secret.

Crew Over 100 crew live onboard the three-storey submarines.

Modern subs rarely have to come up to the surface, except to restock with food for the crew.

Modern supercraft

Nuclear-powered aircraft carriers
Aircraft carriers provide floating battle platforms for planes and missiles. US Navy Nimitz-class carriers are among the largest in the world.

Power Two nuclear reactors.

Weaponry Various missiles, including infra-red homing surface-to-air missiles. Electronic countermeasures for knocking out incoming missiles or planes. Ninety fixed-wing aircraft and helicopters.

Length 332.86m

Crew 3,200 ship's crew, 2,480 air crew.

FUTURE SOLDIER

WHAT'S NEXT?

Here are some examples of equipment, some of it already being tested, that soldiers might well be using in the next few decades.

10

An SMSS vehicle on trial with the US Army.

FUTURE KIT

Exoskeleton suit Soldiers will be able to wear a robotic exoskeleton suit to make them stronger. Sensors in the suit will pick up the soldier's muscle movements and amplify them, triggering the suit's robotic joints to help the soldier pick up extra-heavy loads or move around faster.

Liquid armour Liquid armour is made of fibres that are soft and flexible until they are struck, when they instantly harden. It is much lighter and less bulky than ordinary bulletproof armour, and better at absorbing impact.

Self-healing self-powering uniform Soldiers may one day wear clothes containing an internal power-generation and energy-storage network. The soldier will generate power by moving, and use it to run equipment. The clothes may be made of fibres that can reduce problems such as skin infections.

Robot packhorse Soldiers are likely to be accompanied by robot vehicles, or SMSS (squad mission support systems), carrying food supplies and heavy equipment. The robots will use onboard sensors to help them move across different landscapes.

Extreme bullets New hand weapons include the XM25, a gun that can be programmed to shoot its bullets above and beyond an obstacle such as a wall. Its bullets explode and shower down on the enemy hidden behind. Eventually soldiers are likely to use bullets guided by sensors, currently called EXALTO – 'extreme accuracy tactical ordinance'.

A design for an exoskeleton suit that could protect a soldier in the future.

26

These attackbot prototypes look like they come from a sci-fi film!

Future battlefield

Here is some of the battlefield weaponry already being planned and likely to be available to future soldiers.

E-bombs E-bombs are a futuristic weapons concept currently being investigated. The idea is to generate microwaves over a wide area, destroying electrical equipment such as electronics. The problem still to be solved is how not to damage the equipment of friendly forces. Perhaps unmanned aerial vehicles (UAVs) will carry small E-bomb generators to pinpoint specific targets.

Non-lethal ray gun The US Active Denial System, already being tested, is an example of a weapon that causes temporary pain, making people run away. It produces an invisible low-power microwave beam that causes an instant skin-burning sensation for a few seconds.

Attackbots Robots are likely to be used to fight on the battlefield as well as provide backup for troops. They will be bristling with sensors that enable them to recognise friends or enemies, and cope with different situations.

Optical deception A projection of a hologram, from an airborne projector, could be used to confuse an enemy on the ground for a few moments, distracting them long enough to gain an advantage.

Weather modification A 'weather modification system' could one day be used to alter the weather over small areas, to give advantages to the forces fighting below. Currently it's only possible to seed clouds, to cause rain, but even this limited technology could be helpful in a battlefield situation.

Staying at home With robot soldiers and tanks planned, more human operators will be needed in bases far away from the military zone, monitoring the action and sending commands via computer.

Taking part in future warfare might be more like playing a computer game.

TECHNO WEAPONS

Weaponry of the future is likely to be aimed from space, but attacks are also likely to come through cyberspace. Here are some of the scenarios being discussed and developed.

HYPERSONIC SCRAMJETS

Hypersonic 'scramjet' space planes are likely to travel incredibly fast anywhere in the world to mount an attack or deliver equipment. Super-powerful jet propulsion will enable them to reach low space orbit. A NASA scramjet design is shown left.

Space-based motherships

There are likely to be lots of robots and UAVs on the battlefield of the future, and they could be controlled via unmanned space platforms hovering high above the action. It's possible that such motherships could be used to automatically refuel or rearm UAVs, possibly even beaming laser energy to them.

REFLECTING LASERS

One futuristic idea being explored by scientists is the possibility of directing high-energy laser beams via giant space-based mirrors, perhaps to knock out enemy military satellites or missiles.

Space bodyguards

Space-based platforms such as mirrors and motherships could be patrolled by laser-armed military satellites acting as bodyguards.

Future warfare may be conducted entirely in space, and not on Earth at all.

MAGNETIC SUPERPUNCH

MAHEM ('hydrodynamic explosive munition') is the concept of an anti-tank missile with a powerful magnetic field around it. The idea is that the force of the magnetic field will ram the missile into a target with much more power than today's weaponry.

MICROBOT TROOPS

Microbots – tiny miniaturised robots – could play a part in future warfare, as spies or to disable enemy equipment. Medium-sized minirobots are already used for work such as bomb disposal, but microbots would be much smaller and less easy to spot.

Force fields

Technology has already been developed to create a 'force field' around a tank, using lots of onboard sensors to detect and detonate incoming missiles before they reach the tank itself. Perhaps this concept will be developed to include similar protection for buildings, vehicles and troops.

Fotofighter

A fotofighter is a term for the concept of a fighter jet fitted with all kinds of lasers and sensors, so that it could engage lots of targets simultaneously – perhaps defending itself from incoming missiles while attacking several positions.

CYBERWARS

Cyberwars is the term used for attacking enemy computer systems. Harmful computer viruses can be added by hackers or sent via 'logic bombs', pre-planted during the manufacturing of computer software used in key targets such as power stations or train signals. A cyber-attack could even paralyse a city, knocking out all electronic services. Perhaps the computer networks of the world could turn out to be the main battlefield of the future…

The humble computer mouse will perhaps be the most potent weapon of all in the future.

Aquilifer Soldier who carried a Roman army standard.

Assyrian Empire An empire in the Iraq/Syria region, from 911-605 BCE. Assyrians were noted war charioteers.

Blitzkrieg A tactic used by German forces in World War Two – a fast surprise attack using artillery, planes and tanks.

Cavalry Mounted soldiers.

Centurion Commander of an 80-man Roman army group called a century.

Cornicen A Roman army horn player who blasted out the commander's signals to the troops.

Countermeasures Actions taken to combat incoming enemy attack.

Crenellations Gaps in the top of a castle wall, for aiming a weapon outwards at the enemy.

Cuirassier European cavalry troops, named after their 'cuirasse' breastplates. First appeared in the 1500s.

Cyberwars Attacks on enemy computer systems.

Death ray The name given to a rumoured invention by ancient Greek genius Archimedes, using giant mirrors to focus the Sun's rays, to create fire.

Destrier A big strong medieval war horse.

Dogfight Air combat between two aeroplanes.

E-bomb A weapon that generates microwaves, knocking out electronics.

EXALTO 'Extreme accuracy tactical ordinance', meaning sensor-guided bullets.

Exoskeleton suit Robot-controlled clothing, with sensor-controlled joints, that enhances the strength and endurance of the person wearing it.

Firelance Early Chinese flamethrower weapon using gunpowder.

Fotofighter Term for a fighter jet bristling with lasers and sensors, to enable it to attack more than one target at once.

Gladius Roman short sword.

Greaves Armour shinguards, made of leather, iron or bronze.

Greek Fire A mixture of flaming chemicals used in early medieval warfare.

Head-up display Information projected onto a windscreen, such as the windscreen of a jet fighter.

Hoplite Ancient Greek soldier.

Infra-red sensors Detectors of infra-red radiation given off by objects and people.

Jet propulsion When a machine such as an aeroplane is propelled forward by hot gases shooting out of the back of a jet engine.

Kabuto Japanese Samurai warrior helmet.

Kevlar ™ Very strong fibre used to make bulletproof clothing.

Kusazuri Armoured skirt worn by Japanese Samurai warriors.

Lance Long spear-shaped weapon.

Legate Commander of a Roman legion.

Legion Roman army group of 5,000 soldiers.

Line of battle Naval tactic of positioning warships in a row, to fire broadsides at the enemy.

Liquid armour Armour made of soft flexible fibres that harden when struck.

Mace Iron club used in medieval battles.

MAHEM 'Hydrodynamic explosive munition', an anti-tank missile that uses a magnetic field to give it extra force.

Microbot A miniaturised robot.

Mongols Warrior force who conquered Asia, the Middle East and parts of Europe in the 1200s CE.

Murder hole A hole made in the ceiling of a castle entrance, for pouring hot liquid or dropping stones onto an invading enemy below.

Musket A type of gun which fired musket balls, used from the 1500s to the 1700s.

Night vision goggles Goggles fitted with infra-red sensors, for seeing in the dark.

Normans French-based force which conquered England in 1066.

Onager Giant wooden catapult used by the Roman army in sieges.

Optical deception Camouflage by means of cameras projecting an image of the background onto the front of an object or person.

Phalanx Ancient Greek troop formation, with footsoldiers standing in a rectangle.

Pilum A Roman spear.

Reactive armour Tank armour that can explode an incoming anti-tank charge on impact, before it penetrates the tank itself.

Rifling Spiral of grooves cut inside a gun barrel.

Sabre Large curved sword.

Samurai Japanese warriors, first appearing around the 1200s.

Scramjet Superfast jet with enough power to reach space.

Siege tower Moveable wooden four-sided tower, enabling attacking troops to reach the top of a wall.

Signifer Roman soldier who carried the centurial signum, a spear hung with medallions.

SMSS 'Squad mission support system', a robot that transports equipment for a squad of soldiers.

Spartan A person from the ancient Greek city-state of Sparta, renowned for its brutal military training.

Stealth technology Materials and design used to make a plane or boat as invisible as possible to radar.

Torpedoes Underwater missiles.

Trebuchet A giant medieval catapult used in sieges.

Trireme Ancient Greek war boat powered by oarsmen.

UAV Unmanned aerial vehicle, a remote-controlled plane used for reconnaissance or bombing.

WARFARE WEBSITES

http://www.mesopotamia.co.uk/warfare/challenge/cha_set.html
Become an archaeologist and see if you can find some ancient weapons.

http://www.bbc.co.uk/history/ancient/romans/vindolanda_01.shtm
Find out what it was like to be an ancient Roman soldier far away from home.

http://www.bbc.co.uk/schools/worldwarone/
Listen to true stories about World War One, and plan your own battle strategy.

http://london.iwm.org.uk/
The website of the Imperial War Museums in London.

Note to parents and teachers

Every effort has been made by the Publishers to ensure that the websites in this book are suitable for children, that they are of the highest educational value, and that they contain no inappropriate or offensive material. However, because of the nature of the Internet, it is impossible to guarantee that the contents of these sites will not be altered. We strongly advise that Internet access is supervised by a responsible adult.

INDEX